How to DJ

The Ultimate Guide to Become A DJ

George K.

Table of Contents

Preview Of 'The Ultimate Guide To Starting A Band - How To Start A Band And Be Successful'

Introduction

I want to thank you and congratulate you for purchasing the book, *"How to DJ: The Ultimate Guide to Become a DJ"*.

This book contains proven steps and strategies on understanding and knowing what you need to become a DJ.

Being a disc jockey is all about playing music. Are you interested in becoming one? This book will help you out as this contains information of the different kinds of DJs, plus how each kind functions. You also get to know some of the perks you get for being one.

What kind of personality do you need to have once you become a DJ? Will you need to study certain courses? How will you train? You don't become a good (and popular) DJ without the right skills – phrasing, beatmatching, volume control and equalizing. Find out what they are, as well as their significance in a DJ's life.

Today's DJs need software plus reliable equipment to get them going. Read on to see which software and equipment are recommended for you to use. Beginners will benefit from the guidelines in choosing the proper equipment.

No career has ever been achieved without facing struggles along the way. What problems do DJs have to face, and how were they able to overcome it? What lessons have they learned from it?

Plus, there are tips and suggestions for those first few gigs that you are going to perform.

Thanks again for purchasing this book, I hope you enjoy it!

monetary loss due to the information herein, either directly or indirectly.

Respective authors own all copyrights not held by the publisher.

The information herein is offered for informational purposes solely, and is universal as so. The presentation of the information is without contract or any type of guarantee assurance.

The trademarks that are used are without any consent, and the publication of the trademark is without permission or backing by the trademark owner. All trademarks and brands within this book are for clarifying purposes only and are the owned by the owners themselves, not affiliated with this document.

Chapter 1 – Being a DJ: an Overview

There's more to being a DJ than just playing songs and scratching records. It's also about matching your musical preferences and talents to your audiences' tastes.

It's easy to get started. What's difficult is to be unique and exceptional in a world full of wannabe DJs.

So how do you do it? Read on to learn more.

What Being a Disc Jockey Means

A disc jockey, or a DJ, plays recorded music to his audience. He can play different types of music and use different forms of music playback. It can be as simple as controlling music played in parties, or creating mashups to be played for a crowd.

The acronym 'DJ' is also used as a title of the person who does disc jockeying duties.

A DJ has various duties such as:

- Choose music playlists for a particular event

- Deliver scripted and/or live broadcasts

- Learn different developments in music, as well as in news and current events

- Interview guests, share news and report commentaries

Good DJs are versatile; he should be capable of performing his responsibilities well. Radio DJs, for example, must be willing to coordinate well with directors and technicians for a smooth flow of the show. Guest DJs, on the other hand, should have good people skills for fun interactions with their listeners.

Types of DJs

There are different kinds of disc jockeys.

a. *Radio DJs* – Radio DJs, as implied, work in radio stations. His functions vary; he could give the weather report, or a full-on control of the songs played and broadcasted over AM, FM, internet or digital radio stations.

Famous radio DJs include Russell Brand and Ryan Seacrest.

b. *Mobile DJs* – Mobile DJs (aka wedding DJs) are somehow different from the usual DJs; instead of staying in a particular venue, they travel with their equipment and set-up their systems in varying places. This DJ is more of the entrepreneur type and is DJ-ing for a living.

c. *Club or Bar DJs* – Club DJs use CDs, MP3s or vinyl records and are often found inside clubs, raves and bars. They have different styles and personalities, but they have common goals - to keep the people moving and help maintain the energy of people inside the venue.

d. *Performer or Guest DJs* – These are the more popular DJs; they have established a particular reputation and have earned a number of followers. Guest DJs also function as event hosts and perform in hotels, resorts and other special affairs.

Why Do You Want to be a DJ?

There are many reasons behind wanting to become a DJ. Right now, you have to think and reflect on what your main reason is.

Why do you want to become a DJ? Is it because you want to be famous? Is it because it looks fun and interesting?

Here's something that you have to know – if it's just to be famous, then you'll need to exert twice the effort to be successful. Would you love it enough to have the drive and do the hard work? There's more to being a DJ than fame and fortune; to get there, you need passion, dedication and effort.

You have to love what you do. You have to stick to what you're doing, even if it's difficult, and even if it's challenging.

If you're able to stick with your dreams of being a DJ amidst the challenges, then this could indeed be the career path for you.

Perks of Being a DJ

As an aspiring DJ, you need to find out what's good about being a DJ. What do you get out of it?

You get free stuff. Once you become a well-known DJ, you gain the power to endorse products that you may or may not actually use. One common perk is the clothing endorsement, which is great because you will always have an updated wardrobe as long as you are still relevant to pop culture.

You get assistance from people. As you rise from being an unknown DJ to one who's gradually being known, you'd need a manager to take care of all your scheduled activities. A manager/handler will take care of your flights, check out your equipment, and make sure people behave when they're around you.

You get paid for partying. There's nothing unusual with partying on Friday nights, but in your case, you also get paid for it. You even get to be in charge of the music. That's why DJ-ing

is more than just a job -- you get paid for doing
what you love.

Chapter 2 – How to Get There

The path on becoming a DJ can differ; it all depends on what kind of work are you planning to do as a DJ.

Personality

As a DJ, the most important factor is your love for music. You'd be dealing with music the whole time, after all.

Don't let money be your driving force. If you're just after the money, then you should realize as early as now that you'll have a difficult start. You won't always be paid, especially as a newcomer, until you build a strong fan base. Competition is strong in this career, and there are DJs who are willing to play for free as long as they're given the exposure.

That fan base, on the other hand, won't be built until you know how to interact with people.

You have to learn networking and connecting to your listeners. Your audience will love it if you're able to connect with them, and that if you can radiate your energy to them.

It'll also help to be versatile, adaptable and hungry for knowledge. You have to keep learning and honing your craft to increase your chance for success.

Education

If you're planning to get involved in radio broadcasting, then a good start would be to have a bachelor's degree in journalism or communications.

Enrolling in journalism degree programs will allow you to go for internships at television or radio stations. Internships not only enhance your skills but also give you actual hands-on experience.

Other kinds of DJs usually don't need a specific degree to find work. They learn to be a DJ through self-studying or through being taught by fellow DJs.

Aspiring DJs can also study courses offered by colleges and universities such as audio production, sound engineering and the study of music computer software.

Disc jockeys also wouldn't require a formal certification for work.

Training

To become a radio DJ, you can first start by working for your college radio station. It'll allow you to have experience with the actual equipment but still have the guidance of the seniors if in case you need to ask questions. Plus, it'll help you develop your unique on-air personality.

As an aspiring club DJ, you have to practice a lot. Be familiar with different kinds of technology and mixing tools so that you'll be ready for any malfunctions inside the club or bar. You may need to work first for free, but as long as your heart is in the music, you'll soon improve and be a skilled DJ; the money will soon follow.

How Long Does It Take?

You may need to wait for several years to perfect your skills in being a DJ, especially if you started by taking degree programs that last for four years.

Learning the skills and being known enough to be trusted for jobs can also take a few years more, plus you have to earn more experience and establish your reputation.

Don't rush; give yourself time to become comfortable with what you're doing. Soon, you'll see yourself moving through the tools smoothly, and mixing songs properly.

Chapter 3 – Recommended Software and Equipment

So now you're sure that being a DJ is the right job for you. What's next on your list, then?

Your next step should now be to test the waters and see what you're capable of without making any major investments... yet.

First, download free DJ software so you can try things out.

Recommended DJ Software

You can still be a DJ even if you do not have turntables and vinyl records. Technology can give you the flexibility, cost-effectiveness and convenience through these downloadable programs that can give you an idea of what a DJ does.

Aside from their basic tasks such as loading your music playlists, you use DJ software to apply selected effects and filters, monitor your mixing moves, and perform different cool tricks that wouldn't have been possible before.

- Virtual DJ – DJs can use Virtual DJ if they want to use their computer in playing their music. It offers more options than your typical media player – gives your sounds various effects, plays video and karaoke tracks, organizes your songs, and many more.

- Traktor Pro 2 – This program isn't free, but it offers a free demo version so you can try it out before finally purchasing the full version. Traktor is highly recommended because of its quantization, syncing, and effects. Traktor's manufacturer also offers its own hardware that of course will work best with the software of the same name.

- Mixx – Mixx is an ideal software to use because it works with multiple platforms. It's a well-featured open source program that can already support timecode control. Better yet, this software is free and can work with different DJ controllers and digital music formats.

Software used by DJs usually perform the same tasks, but you can actually be more comfortable with using one rather than the other. It'll help to try out free versions first, and see which ones you find easier to use.

Equipment for Beginner DJs

Now you're on one of the most exciting parts: having and setting up your own equipment.

Find out which ones are the vital parts of your equipment. Learn more about them and understand which ones you should select.

Headphones

A DJ must have headphones. It's a must. It's a need. It's necessary. What's better than a DJ having headphones? A DJ who has a pair of high-quality headphones.

Headphones let you listen to the tracks without the noise from the crowd drowning them out. Like what they're primarily used for – private listening. The more popular ones are Sony, Pioneer and Sennheiser, although more are being added to the list.

Your main concern could be the amount you're willing to spend, especially that you're still a beginner who doesn't have much funds stored (unless you're one of those lucky ones who are prepared to shell out a couple more dollars).

It's not necessary to endorse a particular brand; just take note of these reminders:

- Durability – You'll benefit from having a solid and well-built pair of headphones in the long run; they last longer and can withstand the occasional drops.

- Cable Length – See to it that the headphone cables are long enough because you'll be moving around as you perform your duties as a DJ. Still, it shouldn't be too long that you'll end up getting tangled all over your other equipment.

- Comfort – Choose comfortable headphones; they'll be on your head or around your neck for quite a while.

- Isolation – You're using headphones to isolate your music from the speakers. Headphones with closed backs are good, together with loud and crisp sounds. If you can, test out various headphones to see which ones work the best.

Music

Music is one of the main components of DJing. Today's DJs often use digital music with laptops because it's more convenient and cost-efficient. You don't have to carry records, which are often damaged during transit.

64GB flash disks aren't that expensive, and you can fit more than 16,000 MP3s in it. Most DJs today prefer using digital music because they are more portable, and often sounds better than analog devices.

Finding a store to purchase music from is easy too. Just make sure you'll be buying music of good quality – you wouldn't want to play grainy and distorted music. It'll also help to familiarize yourself with different music genres, as well as get to know more artists so you can build a huge and diverse song library.

Laptop

DJs do not need laptops with high-end specs; they just need to effectively run the software they choose to use. Most laptops released nowadays meet DJing requirements; usual recommended specs include 25GB hard drive space, 2GB RAM, a Core2Duo processor (at the very least), and a couple of USB ports.

Take note of these recommendations for a smoother run.

- Choose laptops that have a good battery life. Most likely it'll be plugged in as you play your music, but having a good laptop battery will ensure a smooth performance in case you do not have access to an available wall socket. It'll also help to have a running battery while on the road just in case you need to listen to music, sort them out and arrange their queues.

- Your laptop should have at least three USB ports. If you don't have three USB ports, then using a USB hub will also work. Why the need for multiple USB ports? This is so that you can plug in your controllers, plus other accessories such as your mouse.

- Your screen should ideally measure 15.6". You'll have difficulty reading songs on a smaller screen, while it might cover you up if you use a big screen.

DJ Mixers / Controllers

Controllers will help you out if you'll be using mp3s and laptops. There are many choices for controllers, so take note of these recommendations to narrow down your search:

- Choose a controller that can be connected through the USB port, as well as one with its own soundcard and audio interface so it'll be easy to use.

- A controller with its own soundcard, separate from the computer's soundcard, will allow you to hear both songs playing on the headphones as well as your main speakers.

- Recommended manufacturers of controllers include Numark and Serato.

- Controllers come with software packages for better chances of compatibility.

Speakers

No one won't hear your music if you don't have speakers. The kind of speaker you'll be using can be based on your DJing level plus the venue or event you'll be playing for.

If you're a beginner, then you can opt for a 2-speaker set that comes with a subwoofer. The subwoofer will be in charge of playing and feeling bass sounds, and this makes it easier for you to beat match.

Got a bigger budget? You can then go for bigger and louder DJ monitor speakers, or choose self-powered ones because they are already tuned, plus they come with built-in amplifiers.

Recommended manufacturers are Pioneer, M-Audio and Yamaha.

You're All Set!

Once you've got all your equipment with you, all you need is to determine your DJ name, and you're all set. Understandably, everything will be quite confusing and blurry, but you can always ask for help from other more experienced DJs and research materials online.

As you get better as a DJ, you can then start investing on better equipment. Better equipment does not immediately translate to being a better DJ, but it'll make you learn more and help you control the music that you're sharing with your audience. You make more people happy and pleased, which is why you wanted to be a DJ in the first place, right?

Chapter 4 – Learning the Skills of DJing

Motivation and drive isn't enough to be a successful DJ. Of course you've got to have the right skills to get you there. Which skills will you need to acquire to perform at your best?

Phrasing

Phrasing is all about mixing songs together, but the songs still end up making sense.

If you have a background in music, then you'll know that songs are composed of phrases structured based on bars and beats.

Songs that you'll be using are almost all in 4/4 time – regardless if its hip-hop, funk, electronic dance music or top 40.

(What 4/4 means is that the song has four beats in one measure, and quarter notes get a beat. On the other hand, 6/8 time indicates 6 beats in one measure and eighth notes get a beat.)

Beatmatching

Beatmatching is all about making the songs you play have the same tempo (i.e. speed the song is playing) as well as phase (i.e. beats' tracks in-time with one another).

Confused? Picture two cars running at the same time. Tempo is when both cars run at the same speed, while phase is when both cars run side by side.

It's done using a pitch fader (for tempo) as well as a pitch-bend button, jog wheel or manual record manipulation (for phase).

Some DJs, however, think that beatmatching is no longer necessary because recent gears already have the built-in sync capability. So the question is: with all the technology incorporated in modern DJ equipment, is beatmatching still relevant? There's already a 'sync' button; why bother learning beatmatching?

It's because learning beatmatching somehow gives you an advantage; it helps you mix almost anything out there. It also helps develop your "sense of sound" – it helps improve your listening skills and helps tune your ears.

If you know how to do beatmatching, you'll know what to listen for. You'll understand which songs are out of tune, when they veer away from their phase, time, etc.

In a nutshell, it makes you become a better DJ, regardless of the kind of DJ you are.

Equalizing

Equalizing, or more referred to as EQing, is done by making frequencies either higher or lower to make songs blend well. EQing won't do magic. What it does is blend two audio signals or more, as well as polish a mixture to become a song that's worthy of listening.

EQing isn't easy; to get you started, remember that most of your space uses up lower frequencies, especially if you're playing dance music. In essence, you don't combine two loud kick drums because they're just too loud to be mixed.

DJ mixers usually have a three-band EQ: either [high, medium, low] or [treble, midrange, bass]. There are mixers that have four-band EQs: high, mid-high, low-mid and low.

Volume/Gain Control

DJ mixers often contain different types of volume control.

- Every channel must possess a gain or trim knob. This allows you to adjust signal levels by checking your meters.

- Line faders adjust signals sent to the main output, which has its own volume control.

- Crossfaders allow you to fade from one channel to the other.

Beginners who don't have their own hardware yet can still get familiarized with these controls through the software they use. Some software programs e.g. Traktor Pro has this 'auto-gain' feature that guides you where you should be if you want your levels match as you fix songs together.

People view volume control differently. It used to be green for go, red is no, yellow is a warning. But since DJs often go to the red zone, manufacturers made it possible for them to reach the red area, but it will still not be loud enough to cause any permanent hearing damage.

In doubt? Then stay in the green. If the music has to be louder, then boost it using your amplifier. Just make sure you don't mess up your signal.

Check your manuals to see how far your equipment can go and learn where the signal can be maxed out.

Chapter 5 – The Challenges and the Lessons

Like any other profession, you're bound to face different challenges along the way as a DJ. It's not an easy path; even David Guetta faces hurdles every now and then.

Plus, you also get to learn priceless lessons that will guide you as you go along.

Learn about the battles fought and the lessons learned by being a disc jockey.

Challenges a DJ Faces

Being a DJ is not a walk in the park; there are times when you have to jump over hurdles to get to where you are, or where you want to be.

There are people who'd disagree with your career choice. Sadly, it could be your loved ones and friends, but they'll soon accept your choice as long as it makes you happy, and that it doesn't harm you a bit. Who knows, you can even have them listen to you as you do your magic.

Equipment can be costly. Aspiring DJs who haven't earned much and don't have a lot of money to start with will find this very challenging. As DJs, you might need to have turntables, digital sound mixers, microphones, music systems and other musical instruments; and these are often expensive.

Every now and then, you're going to play for empty rooms. When this happens, don't dwell on it. Get over it; don't let it rule you. Do you only have a few people listening to you? Still play your heart out. Don't be a mediocre DJ just because you don't have a big audience. Keep your energy levels up, and other DJs, guests and promoters will give you more respect.

You'll get associated with narcotics. As a DJ, you get to be where the wild parties are, and these places are where drug usage and alcohol are both the main concerns. These issues are already being addressed, but still there are people who see DJs not only for the music but also with drugs and excessive alcohol consumption. To combat these wrong impressions, it'll help if DJs campaign against such cool trends, and not to endorse harmful substances.

You have to learn how to balance. As a DJ, you have to keep your audience dancing, but you have to make sure they don't get tired out. You can avoid being boring and still maintain the excitement by learning how to read the crowd. Things getting dull? Raise your beats a notch. Don't worry about it too much, though; you'll learn how to do it and be better as time passes.

Points to Ponder

Being a DJ will also teach you valuable lessons, and some of them will actually work in life itself.

Don't rely on past success.

You might have earned credits to your name, but that doesn't mean you're guaranteed to keep it. You still won't be able to satisfy everyone, and you still have to start from scratch to prove yourself and your capabilities.

It's okay to promote yourself, but make sure to deliver.

Parties won't be too successful without promotion. Send out flyers to people. Take advantage of social media. Promoting yourself is good, but make sure that you'll deliver and back up your promises. If you told people or at least gave them the impression that you're good, then you should definitely be good.

You won't please everyone.

Not everyone will like you. Some will think your music is either underground or mainstream. Some will hate the place and say that it's either too normal or too noisy. Some will hate you and your music just because you haven't fulfilled their request/s.

On the other hand, there are people who'll stick with you not because of your music and/or talent but because of the perks they'll get from you i.e. drink tickets and having the guest list. You tend to tolerate their behavior, but they end up moving to a different DJ once your gigs dry up.

Stay grounded.

Don't let it all go inside your head because if you're not too careful, it'll make you ignore people around you. You'll ignore friendly reminders from people who matter. Your ego will be as inflated as a newly pumped-up balloon.

Learn to accept both criticisms and compliments. Don't think you're good enough that you no longer need to improve. Trust people who matter, as well as their opinions; accept the times when you really stepped up and when you messed up.

Small wins still matter.

Every small victory counts. It may seem like they're worthless, but those victories are what make your success sweeter. Every invitation is a gift; make the most of them.

There are times when you'd take DJing for granted, and that you don't realize how it had become an opportunity to make people happy. Remember that not all people are given the chance to do what you're doing, so keep your head up, and be thankful for your DJing skills.

Chapter 6 – What to Remember During Your First Gig as a DJ

You have now reached your favorite part: playing for an audience.

What opportunities can you take advantage of to show off your skills?

One way you can have people check out your DJ-ing skills is by throwing a house party. You can also try booking professional DJs and introduce them.

If you're more of a mobile DJ, then you can look for special events that you can play for. (Just don't play on too significant events if you're not comfortable yet e.g. weddings.) You can even try out performing for free – just make sure you won't get stuck in that I-play-for-free zone – just to gain experience and to make yourself known.

You also can try handing out business cards and/or demo performances to other DJs, performers, promoters and friends at their events – this will show them that you're willing to support, cooperate and collaborate.

Here are some points to ponder as you perform your first few gigs:

- Show up early. You'd rather be too early than be late. You need time to set up your equipment, plus you'd have to perform sound checks. Having enough time will allow you to determine any problems that may affect the sound of your playlist.

- Make sure the 'regulars' in your frequented venue know you before you approach a promoter or manager formally.

- Don't use equipment that you're not familiar with, especially at the last minute. If you're going to purchase new equipment, then take time to practice using them. Don't break them in at an actual performance.

- As much as possible, don't accept last-minute gigs. Of course every invitation is an opportunity, but you have to remember that as a beginner, you need time to practice your craft. Accept only those that you're sure you can handle. It lessens the chances of you messing up, and you'll end up being known as a DJ who performs well.

- If you've already started establishing a name for yourself, then sell yourself – not just as a DJ, but as a brand.

- Understand that you're playing for a crowd. Prior to your gigs, you might have only played for yourself; hence you play those songs that fit your tastes. Dealing with a crowd, however, means playing for different people with different tastes in music. Learn to accept suggestions as well as criticisms. Use all those for your improvement.

- Always have a Plan B. No matter how careful you are, sometimes things still mess up, and those disrupt or stop your music. Make sure to have a backup plan to ensure smoothness of your performance just in case your original plan doesn't work.

- Keep your feet on the ground and don't let it all go inside your head.

Whether it's your first gig, or you're a beginner who's finally getting around, you can apply the aforementioned tips to make DJing less nerve wracking. Just remember that practice makes perfect, and that you'll only get to practice when you play for a crowd.

Get out there and play your music!

Conclusion

Thank you again for purchasing this book!

I hope this book was able to help you understand what it takes to be a DJ, and what do you need to do so you can achieve it.

Finding out the steps to become a DJ yourself as well as teaching yourself can usually be far more effective than going for a school or classroom for disc jockeys. It'll also help to realize early on what kind of DJ you'd like to become so that you can already set expectations as you trudge that path.

The next step is to apply the steps you've learned in this book. Download the software, be equipped of the skills, hone your mindset and personality, get yourself exposed, and establish a loyal fan base who loves you and your music. Soon, you'll become one of the most popular DJs there is, and we're looking forward to see you shine.

Finally, if you enjoyed this book, then I'd like to
ask you for a favor, would you be kind enough
to leave a review for this book on Amazon? It'd
be greatly appreciated!

Thank you and good luck!

Preview Of 'The Ultimate Guide To Starting A Band - How To Start A Band And Be Successful'

Chapter 1 – The Present Situation of the Music Industry

The music industry consists of individuals and companies that make money by creating and selling music. Among the many organizations and individuals that are working within the industry are the musicians who create and perform the music, the professionals and companies who compose and sell recorded music, those groups that conduct live music performances, agents who help musicians with their music careers, those who broadcast music, musical instrument manufacturers, educators, and journalists.

The music industry became popular in the middle of the 20th century, when records had replaced sheet music as the biggest trend. In the commercial world, people started talking about the recording industry as a loose synonym of the music industry. Together with their many subsidiaries, the majority of this industry for recording music is controlled by 3 major corporate labels – the Universal Music Group, a French-owned company; Sony Music Entertainment, a Japanese-owned recording company; and Warner Music Group, a US-owned company. Independent labels are those labels outside of these three major labels. The biggest part of the live music market is controlled by the leading promoter and owner of a music venue, the Live Nation. It is the past subsidiary of Clear Channel Communications, the biggest owner of radio stations in the United States. The biggest talent management and booking organization is the Creative Artists Agency.

There has been a drastic change in the music industry since the digital distribution of music was launched. A clear indicator of this is the total music sales – since 2000, the sales of recorded music have dropped significantly, while live music or live bands increased in significance. The biggest music retailer in the world today is digital.

If you are interested in buying this book, please

go to: http://amzn.to/23oEMcU

Thanks You!

George K.

Made in the USA
Lexington, KY
06 August 2018